SEX LIVES OF THE POOR AND OBSCURE

Other books by David Schloss:

The Beloved
Legends

SEX LIVES OF THE POOR AND OBSCURE

DAVID SCHLOSS

Carnegie Mellon University Press
Pittsburgh 2001

ACKNOWLEDGMENTS

My thanks to the editors of the periodicals and anthologies where the following appeared, often in somewhat different form:

Antaeus: Key West
Convergence: Midsummer's Eve; A Scene
Crazy Horse: The Crying Room; Sex Lives of the Poor and Obscure
    (as: My Parents, 1939)
Dimensions: West Highland Line
5 A. M.: The Animals; Water Music
The Formalist: The Romantic
The Indiana Review: Blue Pools
Intro: America
The Iowa Review: City of Angels
Ironwood: Father, Dying; Silence
The North American Review: The Anima
Oakwood: An After Dinner Walk
The Ohio Review: A Face Transfigured by Love
Oxford Magazine: A Song of Experience; The Test;
    Testimony of the Man on the Ledge
The Paris Review: Old Collaborators; Tourists Under Glass;
    What the Left Hand is Doing; The White Room; Words
    Instead of a Thousand Pictures
The Partisan Review: The Earthly Paradise; West Texas
Poetry: The Betting Machine that Threw the Big Game; In a
    Blue Light; The Cloak; Figures in the Carpets; The Mind/
    Body Problem; The Poem; Someone Somewhere In Canada
Poetry in the Park: Reunion
Poetry Northwest: A Passionate Friendship
The Seneca Review: Fall in the Park
Shenandoah: "Do Human Babies Need Stimulation,
    Nourishment, Air, Light, Love, Etc.?"
Stardancer: The Apes
Three Rivers Poetry Journal: In Autumn; The Pearl
Western Humanities Review: At "The White Tower,"
    Thessaloniki; Cave Hill; Mapplethorpe On Trial, 1990;
    Visiting Kassandra

Anthology of Magazine Verse & Yearbook of American Poetry,
    1986-8 Edition (Monitor Books, Beverly Hills,
    California): A Face Transfigured by Love
The Beloved (Ashland Poetry Press, Ashland, Ohio):
    A Passionate Friendship
Best of Intro (Associated Writing Programs, Norfolk, Virginia):
    America
Legends (Chapbook—The Windmill Press, Iowa City, Iowa):
    The Betting Machine that Threw the Big Game;
    The Bumble Bee; Someone Somewhere in Canada;
    West Texas
The Literary Anthology (Edinburgh, Scotland): The Apes
The Poetry Anthology (Houghton Mifflin, Boston): The Poem

My thanks also to all the readers who helped me in revising the
poems and preparing this manuscript, especially James Cummins,
James Reiss and Kay Sloan.

The publication of this book is supported by a grant from the
Pennsylvania Council on the Arts.

CONTENTS

For Kay and Signe

Off the side of the crib, a tiny fist:
as you slip closer to look, it's perfect,
with a little philosophy attached to it.

SEX LIVES OF THE POOR AND OBSCURE

[His Parents, 1939]

Through the slippery towns in their costumes of snow,
past Buffalo, frozen as though the icy river
and salt from the highway turning car lights to glitter
had poured over the tops of the houses below,

they arrived at the far end of a distant accord,
just married, exhausted, half-dazed, thinking of all
it took for them to get to Niagara Falls
for what was the dream of their lives in his old Ford.

A bellboy took their baggage to the topmost suite,
where, stalled, they could hear the old awkward murmurs
by the bedside, two unrelated newcomers
asking each other if they should turn up the heat.

Though they could hardly wait for them both to undress,
they'd have a whole weekend to find out whether
they could discover some kind of pleasure together—
or was there something between them first to confess?

Starting with hurried intensity, studied good cheer,
soon they were locked into a kindred point of view
in their shared bed, deciding what or not to do
as prior successful advice filled the heady air.

As sounds seemed to gain power, surrounding the room,
she wondered if there were neighbors listening,
glasses cupped to the walls, to their heavy breathing—
and if she was really ready to go along with him...

If love discouraged her, it wouldn't be absolved,
for she was about to learn how nothing is meant
to be absolutely nothing at all, not resolved
like a falling star in a matter of moments

for a lifetime: thus, during one sleepless night,
she came to determine with all of her might
to make a wish—and she'd have a lifetime to try
to figure out just what it should have been, and why.

THE MIND/BODY PROBLEM

Fox's U-Bet Syrup, Hoffman's, White Rock:
where are the soda pops of yesteryear?
Past torn-down movie houses, culture-shocked,
grey tones of reel-life half-exposed through tears,

he tries to restore all those forts he built
in intervals between the broken backs
of buildings, memories shoring up old guilt
forever leaving him between the cracks:

the works of concentrated hours changed
before his transformation to a ghost
who haunts a neighborhood, dim streets arranged
to never show on film what has been lost.

Now, nothing but the images he keeps
of egg creams and lime rickeys when he can't sleep.

WHAT THE LEFT HAND IS DOING

You wonder if life hasn't already punched
you into its timebound clock often enough
for you to come to preserve a family tree
through the long cruelties of its history.

Can you ever retrieve your parents' lines,
the itinerant and wronged of former times
who found in some daily ritual activities
the only shelter from their uncertainties?

All these acknowledgments of blinded eyes
and constant tragic failures of our lives
to complete themselves in time can't undo
how some end in earth, some in an inferno,

but, living then, you wouldn't have known,
even with freedom, how to write this down.

THE CRYING ROOM

When he was sad, his mother always said,
"If you want to cry, I want you to go
to the crying room." Then he'd walk away,
accepting without protest any place
transformed instantly to four walls, all high
and blank and emptied of her sympathy.

He was oblivious to the shadows
on those walls, the causes of those shadows,
for all the world's wars meant less to him than
chrome throwing back reflections of the beast
he'd become before the machines that loomed
over cracked sidewalks, walking slowly home.

Yet, to the domestic wars of childhood
one day there came a truce, composed in a time
with less to regret. He grew past rage
to a tolerance for what he hoped might last:
the reflective chrome of daylight, so white,
it spilled like milk to fill the killing grounds.

"DO HUMAN BABIES NEED STIMULATION, NOURISHMENT, AIR, LIGHT, LOVE, ETC.?"

You don't need to respond to the question:
you were a human baby once yourself,
you know. So, you know; of course, you know—
but wish the next years something happened, like,
you pushed in a mountain's face, or something.

Yet, when it towered over you and threw
its shadow across your face, did you try
to climb it? At first, as usual, no:
you were still just a baby at heart,
and even needed to befriend that mountain,

its ugly mug. Yet, at the summit, you found
you craved the adulation of the crowd
to fill the thin air at your feet. At least,
that's part of the reason you think you made
the ascent for us in the first place.

So, you were a big baby, after all,
who lived inside a big white house you took
for a mansion—but when you returned
years later, it was just a house, and the rain
blowing through the curtains in the open

windows had ruined all the furnishings.
"Money's no object! Let's leave the heat on
and the windows up," you were almost tempted
to cry. Then, you still thought you needed
to get fresh air and light as you slept

"the sleep of reason," which is, "human childhood,
breeding monsters," as someone famous wrote.
Yes, you read a lot in adolescence
about "the needs of the individual—"
which was, you supposed, yourself, returning

from inspecting your birthplace—which felt
like a museum—with a map on which you stuck
a pin to point it out to us, still wanting
whitewashing, searching for a place in this world.
And, as for those long afternoon naps,

(see "the sleep of reason," above), you gained
some knowledge, slowly but surely, thereby:
very slow, sure, but knowledge, nonetheless,
of sleep itself—as, earlier, you learned
warm milk and cookies in kindergarten...

(No, this won't be a blow-by-blow account
of your growing up: your autobiography
needs to be written, but by somebody else,
who'll love you enough to take it all down—
a need that, once satisfied, might allow you

to pull off the road sometime, to stop
and rest awhile with that girl in your lap,
all stimuli intact—which might permit you
to quit being such a baby about
all this self-regard, in fact, and just stop.)

THE TEST

He knew nothing about the words
that rhyme in English with *nothing*
or *selfish*, the sample questions.

He wondered why he was there then:
there were no words spoken beyond
the fact that they were given time.

Keeping watch, winding up his watch,
he tried to glance at the others,
but saw only objects in space.

Was the waiting, too, a lesson,
motion slowing down to nothing,
as he guessed at the solutions?

Hands thrown around an empty page,
incapable of a gesture
after hours of sample answers,

soon he would no longer know how
to discuss his adolescence
with anyone, with innocence.

A Song of Experience

When the singing white longing came over him,
the swimming, the humming, in gelatinous waves,
they took him aside and questioned him quickly

about nothing, for social security,
as an homage to order, alphabetically:
they wanted him out of their house instantly.

After, on another shore, he remembered
his childhood, so far from that critical womb:
those days he knew nothing, but thought he did;

those days of which he was especially fond.
But why did that little household then appear
the mark of his aspiring? Was it common

to begin his dreams shot out of a cannon,
with no certain passage of time to grow up in?
Did it mean he had to be shot out of himself,

out of fear? At the end of an alley he lay,
completely at one with garbage cans, broken bones,
small party favors, laughed at by children:

there was a continuous beating in his ears,
like the loud flights of steps he had fallen,
the years like a delirium of white noise . . .

Soon he'll be getting ready to move on.
No, nothing has changed: the years are bruises,
his hands in his hip pockets, his head in their hands.

THE CLOAK

As leaves stream out like hair into air
and loam turns to lawns in the spring's
gentle spinning, stripped bark covering
the bare earth as new nourishment, fuel,

Will, the itinerant millworker, returns,
his late father's red cloak on his back,
and birds begin chattering, chiding him
carelessly, as ceaseless as a telegraph.

He wants to tell them how he's been out
carousing for days at sensual festivals,
reprising his previous, generous dreams,

poised for a time when music might stop,
the words intact, still dancing in step
like raw seeds in the hands of the wind.

ON THE STATEN ISLAND FERRY ONE NIGHT

His urge to jump off the back of the boat
into the wake of glittering water
must have been rising before then inside him:
as the windows shone on lower Manhattan,
in the skins of windows he knew confusion,
and was about to call out to her when
he saw the river alive with its lights.

He chased the unfocused words into her lap,
the curve of the smile her belly made
along the crease above her curling hair.
From the nape of her neck, each delicate ear,
she bent circling strands to stroke his cool skin
into wakefulness—the darkness inside him
she'd enter with a darkness of her own.

All through the night their faces were bent
to their bodies' tasks, rocking back and forth
between two islands, riding the dark waves.
As he lay on his back, she felt as warm
to him as his cock, waking into her mouth
as she let her breasts fall from her clothes,
catching his breath as the salt liquid flowed . . .

Beyond that time the lights have been dimmed,
the shades have been drawn, the air become filled
with their tentative confessions of love.
Nothing may come of this—but radiance,
or forgetfulness—so they leave it awhile,
like that boat plunging on through the night,
its lights dimming only into the dawn.

THE ANIMALS

The boyfriend feels daring enough to stand
inside the teenaged daughter's open door
and make her play the music he demands,
which she pretends she's never heard before.

Her father betrays his trade as a actor
by standing out on the streetcorner then
and not even getting paid as an extra
in the film he doesn't know that he's in.

He thinks, "Just as you begin to get it, pal,
it gets you. After the first woman fell,
mankind fell into complicity with lust.

No longer could they be trusted to trust
to certain feelings, the straight, the true—
like tamed animals in an unbridled zoo."

FATHER, DYING

No, it's not like snow on snow falling,
your dying, wanting to be held by us
in an inhuman cold you wish could be
melted before they come to parcel out
the parts of your body . . . will we help?

You know we can't, yet promise anything,
because you've spent these days like a snail,
bones curling tighter, setting together,
the pulse at your wrist pale as the bracelet
a nurse wound around your whitened fist.

Now, when you wake, hot sleep's fallen open
like a robe flung over your face, the hours
when you glow like coal in a fireplace,
adding something to the long list of things
you know you'll never tell us about . . .

But there's a new surge of breathing soon,
called forth from branches of lungs that twist
your tongue into an awkward muffled prayer
for us—once you're too weakened to speak—
to sacrifice you to the blinding air.

CAVE HILL

It rained the day we came through there to see
if someone you were named for could be found:
stones formed a kind of sculpture garden; trees,
dimmed figures standing quietly around.

The graves of children guarded by the fine
white wings of angels sweeping heavy air
spread to enclose us in the formal lines
of generations fixed beneath their care.

Your face was lost in thought above the plans
our family lived and died within, each plot
of ground kept up by numberless numb hands
now buried there, names lost to time—but not

our lineage: one vein in the mass of grains
of marble stained beneath the blurring rain.

BLUE POOLS

You know in what drawer the keys to my door
are kept, and what you do or don't do with
such information doesn't just happen:
we participate in love's flowing, coming
and going by acts of desire alone.

We can place calipers on any two parts
of our two bodies and get a different
sense of our stories merging variously
into a whole: ravelled out, coming clear,
our complexities are complementary.

Either we're happy or we're not, but if
we try to fake it, we'll still have to live
with the truth of liquid pulsing in the tides,
the discord it makes of the moon's illusion
of comfort at the center of the sky.

You hold up some spray, white hands full of spray,
which ebbs, slips away, as winds blow the black
sky blue again, your eyes now restoring
and reflecting the sky in its softening—
the idea of blue swimming into pools—

as the sun begins swimming into you.

The Pearl

The sky trembles, grey,
an irritation that may
produce some new pearl:

for now, all the world
lies naked to the rain
before it shines again

as translucently clear
as sun through the air.
Then, there's more room

inside this bright room
we rest together in,
wedding skin to skin

as a pearl lustrously
forms its own clarity
into one body and warms

the world within our arms.

KEY WEST

Upon this imaginary island
the only thing constantly threatened
is the thought of becoming ourselves:
"I used to smash at mirrors," one says,
"wishing I could make myself more young."

Yet, made with a gift for gleaning truth
from the syllables of common speech,
with its insecure authority
a jukebox speaks to us through the walls
of passions torn from the passing years:

weaving our own soft shrouds of rhetoric,
stalking the dark air for its music,
from this position we get along only
with those who choose us, those we've chosen,
thus belonging in some sense to a "crowd."

We enter into one another's dance,
trying to find some direction or sense
to lives we once publicly disowned,
so we might discover, entranced, beyond,
the loves of a new generation.

So our pasts may be fully abandoned,
we lock ourselves into others' hands—
or, never having felt inside, express
desires, disaffections, with disgust,
driven as if by a matter of course

to lust as part of our everyday lives,
continuing to resign ourselves
to landscapes full of holes, over which
houses are built, new battles are fought,
bone resting on bone, as if there's no choice

on this vast salt plain beneath humped hills,
foundations resting on similar wills,
connections that bind bodies into knots,
thick blankets of smoke, explosions floating
in still wakes through all our emotions.

There's so little to do during the days
stretching out, surrounded by waves,
when someone makes up a new line, a new lie,
we all go down to the docks to watch
the fresh fish imagery swimming by:

anxious to reproduce an ancient rite
beneath the sun flaming its dying light,
belittling our little epiphanies,
we become like born-again Christians
working to believe in a miracle.

The muscles at the backs of our necks
twitch at each pulse of sun as it sets,
surrendering at last to dead calm,
the pervasive hum—that's all there is—
bathing our bodies in sinking feelings.

MIDSUMMER'S EVE

If we were farther north
the sun wouldn't set,
but here its disk

is already sinking,
burning to illuminate
the lucid lake.

No moonlight falls through
the cracks in these walls,
no breezes tonight—

though the dead cells
of the wood seem to breathe,
and the mouths of streams

which feed the lake,
like our mouths, flow away
into darkness, a wilderness

which invites us
to open ourselves instead
of holding in this cabin

to the lesser stars of day.

BLACK LAKE

By that lake, couples lie
in love with the dark
stirring, beguiled by waves'
mortal motions—some youths
and the moon, wish-fishing.

Oil's forming everywhere—
in the xylems of extinct
planted systems; skin; hair—
as though each new leaf of
their life's deeply breathed.

Soon the lovers will lift
soft fabrics from the limbs
they desire to cover as
their own encyclopediasts
without encyclopedias . . .

Their desire's for a kind
of justice: old mistakes
revoked or rectified in
some happier world where
all former lives are crushed.

IN A BLUE LIGHT

From one point of view, you're nothing
    but the blood coursing through
your brain as you begin to fall asleep,
    floating away on that stream;
you dream of a black and white weather
    where air takes the shapes of
a Beethoven figure, a violent concerto,
    everything starting to storm.

Some headlights up ahead on the tracks,
    in a fugue by another composer,
form a crossroads, which you might take
    to follow its uncertain fate:
your face of opposing tensions depends
    on memory of a childhood place
that feels, at once, full of everything
    yet nothing you've ever known.

How much yearly debt to this landscape
    do you owe, a city that draws
its own cup of poison, its eerie green
    lights like galaxies of stars?
Walking home across the humming bridges
    beyond wrath or old invective,
you search the garrulous and sedentary
    remains for humane enterprise.

Now, your family bids you welcome back:
    someday you'll be buried here
with them, yet can't escape its paradox
    about the decent thing to do,
sitting in the glow of yellow lamplight
    wishing you could be different,
deciding what you want to contribute to
    the lost culture of the group.

Theirs was one working class initiative,
    lucky words carrying them past
old inequities and dumb animal cunning,
    a long journey made resolutely:
they feel no need to shed the ignorance
    ringing with false insouciance,
nor break up the old household, even if
    they must lock its glass doors.

Powerfully determined, their habits form
    patterns of their life beneath,
which you re-enter, the mover, the shaker
    of aged heads of the oblivious,
light returning your own gaze that keeps
    a form of nightmare insistence,
cold laws, which for some moments become
    all you feel, all you can know.

Will they let you build your own statue
    to dawn beyond their seasonal
careenings towards winter, now pulling
    you down around their waists?
Being born seems just another old story
    as shadows move in low relief:
Answer all the questions we put to you,
    they say, *with purity of heart.*

As politicians must hide their motives,
    you lie deep inside your skin,
its uncertainty of innocence betraying
    the independence you craved:
you'd reassemble the dissembling house,
    giving up its striking denials,
to save one old couple, trapped inside
    the genealogy of the wallpaper.

This world's filled with so many holes,
　　each collecting a share of snow,
what looks like abandoned mattresses in
　　moonlight are objects of decay
fitting themselves to nightmarish masks,
　　folded up dreams closing around
the words you haven't wrung out as yet,
　　old stubbornness inside a mine.

One old couple shuffles past the rusting
　　plants, her hand on his shoulder,
broken machinery unveiling itself within
　　pervasive blue and failing light:
like so many others, they woke too late,
　　long after giving up their lives
to the dream manipulations of the world
　　you carry still inside your head.

MEMORIAL

We were living in an abandoned theater
long past repairing, or much fixing up—
we couldn't afford it—although the space,
commodious, ornate, peeling walls rising
over forty feet into velvet gloom,
made a kind of burned-out heaven: dull stars
swirled into plaster, painted on the ceiling.

Beyond the marquee with its missing bulbs,
the room was so huge we could keep old cars
inside, off the busy streets, pitch a tent,
and camp among remains of fallen marble.
Asleep on concrete slabs, with rugs, in rags,
we'd feel snug somehow surrounded by holes
in boarded up windows leaking wintry light.

Someone we loved, a famous rock musician,
we once were told, had killed himself on stage
with a knife to his throat: he was angry at
a friend of his, but turned it on himself.
He used to play for crowds at concerts there,
but that place, once his, was ours then, alive
still in our bodies, needing no repair.

THE BETTING MACHINE THAT
THREW THE BIG GAME

In the good old days, whenever a husband
suspected his wife of some carnal betrayal,
he returned to prior infidelities:
thus, the idea of marriage was maintained,
the possibility of the household sustained.

Now, we know, no such simple scruples remain:
in our current domestic penal system,
every penny betokens a lack of want:
with TV dinners set before a TV set,
anything that moves, well, we'll condescend to it.

But a man is a malleable object,
a beacon to his past: so, when one computer
carries a bit of knowledge into the next room
where the other computer is masturbating,
either may choose to faithfully refuse to think nothing.

AT THE END

"The head sat like a little hat
at the end of an enormous cock,"
she said, to make him jealous: how
she used to turn her husband on.

He had enough hard knowledge then,
all he needed to imagine them—
though lust, their therapists agreed,
in the end, results in *liebestod*.

Still, no one else could show him how
to stretch his arms beside his head
without shaking, yet not shake off
the pangs that pierced the viscera.

No choice, because he couldn't choose
which head he'd use to reason with
beyond the things she told him, when
things were the way they had to be.

THE ROMANTIC

That old life of romance and loving women
is over—starting up again—is over:
he feels disabled, as, formerly, in freedom,
he tried to think of something else besides her.

He reads his history, and sleeps, and dreams
her floating face—which keeps returning, worse,
to launch a thousand images—a sea that seems
unbounded while still bound, a universe,

disordered, roiling; reconstructed, free
from such romantic high intensity
that led him to exhausted shores to try
to rest—yet resurrects his dying sighs,

which led him once to think he might erase
what he can not: the memory of her face.

REUNION

He ran into his wife of many years,
ex-wife he hadn't seen for many years,
struck shyly dumb when they both stood before
the Rembrandts by accident in the mile
of museums kept open one night. He smiled,

and started talking, hoping for the best,
inside another, still-familiar sense
of rhythms fixed till death, their jumbled plans—
before they grew to see each place they knew,
or once just fantasized about, as lost.

"I've thought of you—a lot—" she said. "Me, too."
"Yes, I know—" with that typical mystical
expression in her eyes. "If I just need
to think of you for you to know, I'd say
that we can always keep in touch this way."

She laughed, the same old look of recognition,
as when they, once upon a time, were close,
when looks were still enough to keep them close;
then turned, as lovely as in memory—more—
time turning, turning back to innocence,

before they knew it couldn't last, before . . .
His heart didn't break—but he was afraid
of the strangeness when they each turned away
like the two nervous children, twenty always,
who married each other for life one day.

AN AFTER DINNER WALK

He descended into a darkness suspended
beyond his reach, drifting, shivering beneath
a fine rain he could sense only by touch,
passing bare houses with unlit porches,

detached garages, tidy fenced-in yards;
then, unpaved streets, rough-boarded sidewalks,
new construction, foundations laid out
in squares, like great holes within the dark.

He wandered, to stand at last at a crossing
with stirred pools of water reflecting back
pieces of light at the sides of wet tracks

as a long train flashed across the mud flats,
forming its own stretched-out horizon,
"Great Mid-Western," slowly passing, then gone.

WEST TEXAS

They pitched about like tumbleweeds,
until she blew into his arms.
Next day she saw him, newly wed,
holding heavy stones in his hands:

he kneaded sand like a surgeon
of water on the flat, dry land,
in all the holes picked clean of stones,
removed, then rolled back over them.

Then he leapt up and bought a cow:
on its back the ticks went flying,
like thoughts behind his dusty eyes—
but still there was something missing . . .

In an aura of late pale light,
she found herself widowed one day,
family albums, treasures buried
within a secret bureau drawer.

She lived on alone, devoted
to the fields he'd planned on planting
beneath a sullen solar wind,
soil released from desiccation—

until, flowering, in that bowl
hung from blue sky like a ceiling,
cast in its glow, there were shadows
of clouds she could enter again.

ILLUMINATIONS

Dürer painted a plain desk pushed against
a bare church wall, yet etched a tuft of grass
with no detail left out: it's what he thought
Jesus meant when he said, "I am the Light."

Since sight's magnet was the source of his art,
he often felt moved by little captive flecks
of paint's need for flesh, expressing its life
as primal matter sang, "Let there be light!"

Dürer, young, adorned himself with flowers
for a self-portrait aimed toward timelessness
through time, but lived to see the finest lines
would craze across the canvas of a face.

He sketched those enveloping lines around
other lives and deaths worth noting, showing
how flesh could burn, inflamed with inner light
on each thought displayed, warmed by a forehead.

In his portrait, Luther's like a smoothed prune
in a play of pity: though no tongues of flame
lap the dark background, there's little doubt
the Devil found his figure in that gloom.

THE APES

Next day, the men looked up
as if the sun had struck them
down: they had been with the apes.

The apes smelled like wet blankets
in the rain, wet woolen blankets,
and as tame as any man.

The naturalists loved them
for their humanity—their own,
naturally—better than men.

City of Angels

They hang around their living rooms
to flash points of dullness, dryness
covering the outsides of their houses
when Santa Ana winds begin to spread,
enough to smother every nodding head.

Though leisure plays important parts
in all their lives, after they stare
for awhile into their own blank palms,
they come flying down their mountains
to show off their new accumulations.

Nothing less need be done to impress
the waiting populace below than this
display of richness: thick exhausts
floating from tailpipes, the effluents
and white residue of their affluence.

"If something dies, just let it be,"
they say, "let the sleeping dog lie,"
even as their dirt blows back to dust
or turns into blackened balls of mud
under the fire departments' floods.

For, if their waste scatters like ash,
still, it is theirs, from higher up
the hills now burning like kindling,
remaining always threatened by fires,
yet never consumed, like their desires.

SOMEONE SOMEWHERE IN CANADA

The bad years seemed over at last as she flushed
her past life like a fetus down the toilet
and entered America. She threw her old clothes
into an incinerator on the way out;
she came in singing before the new laws.

She could afford to, gaining an extra dime
for each dollar she had, coming to Chicago—
until one day she woke to find herself stripped,
lying drugged and raped on a cold windy street,
crawling beneath a row of parked cars to keep warm.

For years she'd lived a life without feeling
in the present, passing no judgment, dreaming
only of some more comfortable future.
But dreams couldn't save her from what she did then:
she slit her wrists, she cut her belly open.

Her will was broken with the first hard touch
of the future she thought she'd escape, going back
north again on the bus, trying to resurrect
the familiar earthen colors, hoping they might
still remain neutral as her low spirits fell.

Almost there, she checked into a motel;
at the edge of the bed she sweated and trembled.
The pool, the barroom beckoned, dark lit fishtanks—
so she drank . . . She must have gotten very drunk,
because, when she woke, she remembered nothing.

Then the old sense of abandonment returned,
and remained as she lay stretched out somewhere between
Winnepeg and Sasketoon, reborn again
to the same physical facts: there on the nightstand
someone had left her a small pile of cash.

STUDIO 54

As the dancers at The Studio,
  with painted faces bared,
passed by in one old video
  melting into murky air,

the camera crept still nearer
  the center of the dance,
and we became the secret sharers
  of style's impermanence.

Listening past the hectic music,
  we heard one beauty say,
"All this glitter for the public
  is only death at play."

Rinsing color from their faces,
  smoke pressed upon them, gone
by the hour of confirmation
  of the coming of the dawn.

Then we saw each dancer frozen,
  escaping that hard floor;
the seals of skin remained unbroken,
  but nothing was restored.

As bodies merely turned to bodies,
  "The flesh melts," we inferred,
"through the turnings of the years
  what remains is only words."

And the vastnesses of days
  stretched like drifting sands
to the writing on this page,
  lines ending in our hands.

TESTIMONY OF THE MAN ON THE LEDGE

"At the frozen start of yet another year,
all senses absent but that of absent pain
for one life ending, one beginning again,

since there's only this one world we have,
we must learn to work within its system,
suffering all the sincere stupidities

of men and women, who we'll come to love—
or, if we fail, some others form a jury
of our guilty consciences for all the years

that should have meant something else or more
than a face of raw skin, a mask worn within
public restrooms with polished marble floors,

bare whitewashed walls, fast becoming empty
when we'd emulate the arsonists and light
a match; another; then another one—

if only to admire each flaring's calm result,
our contempt like that ash, still crumbling,
left behind, defining our cold extremities.

Yet, addicted to heat, we'd group our needs
with those who hold abuses of their lives
withering within their own dangling arms,

fire feeding on meat clear through to the bones,
which come to rest at last on rusty hooks . . ."
Before bystanders' deep deliberate stares,

he leans off the ledge into the moon's eye,
becoming more and more enormous at the end,
giving no answer to the simple ways of men.

A Face Transfigured By Love

Perhaps in the office of a public building,
down a long fluorescent-lit corridor, one night,
with soft straight light brown hair with red highlights (his type),

she'll sit waiting for him, combing out her long hair,
one leg carelessly flung over the side of her chair,
slowly pushing herself across the slick waxed floor.

Beyond that world of new bodies to be explored,
it's raining outside; soon the others will go home
with their dates for the night, and they will be alone.

In still another private undress rehearsal,
he sets forth on a ritual inches-long journey
into the deepest dream of his necessity—

until, coat collar turned up, stomach upset,
he slides through the shadows, her silent escort,
along wet sidewalks lit only by the panes

of those public buildings' windows dimmed by rain,
reflecting back to him all his fears as he runs
into the center of darkness from which he comes.

LIVES OF THE POET

Sometimes he feels like the boss of a gang of misfits
shovelling load after load after load of useless shit—
or, it's like being gunned down in an elevator
simply because he happens to go down in it later
with some strangers some other stranger wants to gun down:

that sort of incremental bad luck. Like the time he had
an incidental fuck with a married woman, so bad,
she was turned on only after the fact by her guilt about
their "doing it." In each case, he feels innocent without
any pleasure, finding himself in the wrong time, wrong town—

as now he finds himself teaching creative writing,
a long chain of inconsequential and unexciting
events adding up to the life he'd use as an example
for a class full of strangers "exercising their potential,"
waiting to be gunned down as soon as they try to fly

the mundane atmosphere of the collegiate corridors.
When he's done teaching, his "elevator to the stars—"
a phrase he heard for the first time when using "poppers,"
Amyl Nitrate, meant to clear the lungs of asthma sufferers,
but taken then with some friends of a friend to get high—

he'd reproduce that "high," a quick ride to delight,
with the students he happens to find at his door each night,
lungs tingling from breathing the heady musk of their flesh.
Is that what his would-be higher criticism of sex
would be: delight ever after? Not quite. In fact,

his stream of higher consciousness floats him only so far,
to the pitfalls of peaceful occupation in time of war,
the deferment for "essential literary employment"
he got by avoiding any sort of commitment
to any sort of regular work by becoming a poet.

So, he tries the innocent bystander bit at first,
standing around feeling uncomfortable after the worst
has already happened: student bodies piled on the floor,
heads mangled by the relentless elevator doors
banging back and forth against their skulls like the voice

of the instructor before them; like the back and forth choice
between him and some of them, reverberating with pleasure
in his ears, even though his mind was often elsewhere . . .
"Don't you feel exquisitely guilty?" that wife had said,
the consequences anything but casual inside his head—

as he says it again, to his students, who don't really care
how, years later, he realizes his answer, "Well, yes,"
was formed like the facts of his life by what he only guessed
he chose at random at the time—the evidence of his own loss
of innocence—as he prepares to give another class

of strangers another lecture about his guilty failure
to use his guilty failures as a subject for the theme
of guilt, for them to hand in as a story or a poem,
for example: a portrait of the artist indicting
himself as a teacher of a class in creative writing.

At The Grave Of D. S.

He knew nothing about it
until a friend mentioned it,
who said he cried over it
on his way to the dentist,
where the upkeep of his teeth
was slowly killing him.

The fact of that cenotaph
struck him as funny at first—
then he thought about the costs
adding up: a plush plot
inside a traffic island
in midtown Manhattan.

As a marker, off the street
between Park and 33rd,
someone had nailed to a post,
"Here D. S. lies/in his words."
With the upkeep of that spot
he felt more and more interred.

THE BUMBLE BEE

He is our good fellow: for he would take
the flower of innocence for his meal;
for he would climb the stem of folly;
for he can make the angry poppy happy;
for he does not bow before the mighty;
for he climbs, yet still remembers grace.

And when he sups, he lets dead meat lie—
in which he imitates the humming bird,
and thus maintains an image of the Lord
of Those That Fly: in his yellow jacket,
divesting himself of pollen's sweet pretense,
he digests gardens and acres thereby.

For he will fly in any weather, blind—
for he flies both straight and narrow;
for by his flight he signals his kind.
His stinger may be deadly as an arrow,
but he will bear nectar and no malice,
and so he benignly forbears to sting.

But should he sting, he dies for shame,
buzzing loud against the injustice—
for he needs no defense but himself,
and no other reason to be than the air,
leaping meadows, leaving what he takes
better for his gently being there.

A ROYAL FABLE

[Charles and Diana]

As children's entertainments bear the fruits
  of grown-ups' mostly practical pursuits,
total freedom can lead to total misconception:
  she offered herself up to his inspection
as a diagnostically perfectly innocent person;
  he moved and reproved her with his caution.

He marked his boundaries then with a fine mist
  and wore a special mask in which he'd kiss,
as if going down, deep underground, like a mole
  pleased to turn packed earth into new holes.
But, coming up for air, tempting their fortunes,
  soon enough, they would exchange positions.

A sensitive follower at first, just a commoner,
  implicitly there like the crowds, a blur
walking behind him in the shadows, yet serene,
  she knew what it meant for her to be seen
with him as she knew the glory of a future king
  turning back to offer her a wedding ring.

Once, he'd benevolently counted her footsteps
  as blessings, two at a time, faster clips
up the stairs—but he began to feel too harried.
  If they stopped, he knew, they'd be married,
like an unwitting team of long-tethered animals
  working together for life, as in fables.

LOCKER ROOM

Varieties of cocks, of course, at first;
then, steamy camaraderie, reeks of sweat—
but fewer jokes are told than you'd expect—
as if, casual, mirrored, nakedness reversed

the sense that flesh gone long without wants art:
pale bodies flushed, tanned, smooth, slim, rippled, fat,
displayed for eyes to touch, or be touched at
the faces torsos make of disembodied parts.

How solemnly sad these figures seem inside
exclusive masks of skin, tattoos like veils—
bold yet shy, veined muscles trembling—too frail
to face the showering world naked as brides:

Life's love letters once came signed, *Sealed With A Kiss;*
these envelopes now just glazed with its spit.

UR-CURMUDGEON IN HIGH DUDGEON

He's never had enough time off
to know what tension it exacts
to keep his screwed-up views
of the universe intact:

his faith's to disbelieve
in whatever he perceives
as just another wretched story
as written by O. Henry,

a manipulative surprise:
he wants to know what he'll eat
at the bottom of the box—
the trick or the treat?

He thinks he thinks like a god,
and likens what things we lose
to hard crossword puzzle clues
about life's difficult facts,

as if being a critic means
that others' acceptance
would be a kind of comeuppance,
the scorning of his scorn:

"We're all born," he insists,
"between the piss and the shit."

NATHAN THE WISE

Who is Nathan in our lives,
  and why are we in his?
He wanders closely at our sides,
  among old friends and wives,
forever ready to chastise,
  predicting rainy weather,
bunions under leaking leather,
  toadstools like beach umbrellas.

Philosophizing Nathanness,
  he waits for our mishaps,
for us to come to him, perhaps,
  and lay ourselves prostrate
at the very feet of the state
  of depression he creates,
an Inquisition of the Obvious
  all our days around us.

What is this Nathan who sits
  on every head like lice?
A brooding bird ready to shit
  or lay eggs down the faces
that won't face the bad advice
  he fills with commonplaces,
skulking into darkened corners,
  demeanor like a hired mourner's.

Are the poor in spirit ever thus?
  A sister's lover's elder brother,
dripping with self-righteousness
  demanding special recognition;
the second son of our mother's
  most distant second cousin,
he comes to visit and commit us
  to taking care of him—for good?

Surrounding us in his Nathanhood,
  he lights the neighborhood
with triumphant despair, the air
  filled till we no longer care
how all he says seems guaranteed
  to cause some inner strife
or engender the greater danger
  of unrelieved anger for life.

Then he almost fades before us,
  transpiring into nothingness,
good senses squandered on moments
  as full of holes as doughnuts:
he'd eat each heavy, greasy thing
  to the promised inner ring—
or, going further, find his own
  road to perdition back home.

Let someone else sing the praise
  of Nathan, the true-blue guru
who would lead us beneath the new
  wet blankets of our days—
woven for a lost tribe of Nathans
  achieving their own nationhood
under one flag, a vacuum of good,
  invisible, with nothing for all.

POET IN RESIDENCE

As prima donnas greet their coteries
with patent greasiness, he grasps the sense
from all his rapt, devoted votaries'
impatient pants, and swells his audience
with little licks for each one as he goes
aloft amidst the crowd, which, amplified
in limp compliance, reaping what he sows,
hopes he'll score the thickness of their hides.

He's up on stage now: something's up his sleeve,
as, eagerly, hordes grovel for his words,
suspending thought for magic to believe
and follow, like deep shovels, shallow turds.
Applause is food transformed to shit in him,
or fat around this sack of guts whose *mots*
reduce potential wit to gossip, grim
flat verbiage, his verse phlegmatic prose.

Yet, every class's center of attention,
self-conceiving hero, must be on the top:
his pounding erudition presents pretensions
they can't see through to watch the trousers drop,
and recognize, revealed, the naked ass,
black hole at the very center, stands alone—
the infinite expansion of the gas—
until his meager point gets driven home.

This man of few ideas, who'd gladly teach,
thin meanings cut as by Exacto knives,
redeeming insignificance, can't reach
inside the heart, or semblance of our lives:
"You must orbit in my circle, or be damned!"
His narcissism mines its own displays
of "gems," a semi-precious flim-flam man
whose main accomplishment's to keep it up for days.

Mapplethorpe On Trial, 1990

Around men's butts bluenoses sneak a sniff,
outside academies of arts—old farts
aspiring to be shits—protesting as if
they never fucked, or lusted in their hearts.

Coy conversations start, fueled by "the facts"
they gather from what cops saw in bare skin,
rough trade balanced by unbalanced attacks
in courtrooms where little light filters in.

The cool surfaces of "pornographic" works,
their orchestrated textures, become cartoons
removed from contexts of his life by jerks
of the adversarial, the opportune,

who have no cause beyond "the evidence"
they use to turn away from hard content—
hard acts to introduce in his defense
from their version of vision as excrement.

We'll wash all the dirt out of our hair,
falling for weeks from the soundbites they blurt,
kept alive by media full of hot air,
before everyone's nailed, jailed, or just hurt—

for, if one side languishes, the other one,
as their violent remonstrations demonstrate,
will organize and aim their phallic guns
as opposition clarifies their hate.

FAILURES

"Hosannas to those who have failed!"

He has friends, but only in low places
in the city of the suspiciously happy
where he's for hire, his lucky charms

at his throat, asking, *Where's the key?*
of new customers who'd use their tiny
silver spoons, trying, high, to fit in.

To them he provides an unreliable guide
to greater pleasures in gilded mirrors
they suck from, holding lessening lines

of fallen snow within those small hours
that create strangeness from sameness,
whittling them down to size, so, later,

releasing all of their uncaged images,
they won't even try to be recognized.

A SCENE

The old drunk in the laundromat
leaps into the sheets. "Sort him out!"
shout the wives of the neighborhood.

He comes out dressed in infant's wear—
yet, whatever he slumps into
looks tired, even the plastic chairs.

Frozen in alcohol, his women
and children all gone when we wakes,
what language is left to him then?

As he leaves, the windowpane shakes.

ANOTHER MODEL YEAR

As dank smells waft from a street that reveals
the bad taste of builders and neighbors anew,
you feel you'll never see the last of that love
for congealing displays of dissembling decor:
bric-a-brac, gingerbread, fake tar-paper bricks,
siding peeling off in strips, thickening over
layers of dust on top of paint on top of grease.

Beyond rest those species of rusted automobiles,
bodies up on blocks, dulled by seasons of salt
to their permanently dirty, flat, matte finish,
upholstery musty, shredding, nicotine-infused,
with some thin nostalgias rising to the nostrils
of those who've long since forgotten the thrill
of ownership from when those cars were still new.

Younger, you used to stare at yours by the hour
from a second-floor apartment window, thinking,
"That's mine—those clean bright successful lines—"
but now, parked in your yard, it's an admission
of defeat, proof that you can't afford to think
anymore of how you might never afford another—
becoming more and more like a silent partner:

always in the background, yet never spoken of—
with that sickly green it shares with the walls
like a correlative of neglect, playing its part
in the scene until there's no desire left to take
those wheels out for a spin—ignored as you now
ignore the advent of each model year, the new
flourishing beyond the ruins of another life.

AMERICA

"The biggest engine made,"
he said, and all night passed
the slower trucks along the way.

Inside the cab, snow, light,
fell around his clear head
from the distance of no night's sleep.

The early morning fog
covered the ground, white fur,
like a first deer at a deer crossing:

"There's a lot of snow at the heart,"
he said, "friends to drive with . . ."
Then: "This is where we live."

A PASSIONATE FRIENDSHIP

Like a father to a son,
like a son to a father,
they constantly changed
what they were to each other:

first one, then the other,
began to go somewhere,
held open a door
to some glorious future,

then politely stepped back
and bowed low to the other,
who in turn stepped forward
before returning to where

the first one stood waiting,
as polite as the other.
For neither would ever
pass into the future

unless both went together—
and as they grew older
they saw death from afar,
a mysterious door

they could never quite enter—
and so they remained,
rehearsing together,
rehearsing their pleasure,

so much did they care
for each other.

FALL IN THE PARK

As a man bestows a kiss
upon the head of a child,
he thinks that their leaves
must all soon die

and the trees don't care;
then, he thinks of all
the little cancelled dresses
among the colors.

Now he is leaving the park,
as police enter the leaves
to find bodies for which
they've been searching the city.

The moon rises, at sunset,
like the girl pulled
from the lake in the park
by her hair, from the dark

waters beneath the day:
in cold comforting light
red waves rapidly break
the dominance of night.

WATER MUSIC

[A. Hitler and E. Braun in their bunker]

Before she can give him some incontrovertible
diagnosis of his taste for abuse, as a music lover
    sometimes breaks in half a record he's bought
and brought home to play in his enthusiasm to hear it,
    now he bends her over his knees and delivers
a back-breaking spanking in his excitement to see her.

When he strips her, beyond the old Naked Maja effect,
    she reminds him of a little girl he once knew,
a bad hairless-bodied little Jew, crying as he hit her
    for breaking his record of *Tubby The Tuba:*
she sat on it, as now he sits on her, ready to break
    into tears or laughter at her tears any moment.

Since she sings like a child inside her firm flesh
and he's a collector of songs, this is a musicological
    activity, he reminds her, tying her up, turning her
around, checking for scratches as he goes for the record
    with his hard metal ruler, taking out on her
all his feeling for pain and pleasure together . . .

She's lying on a package he brought down from the shelf
    all this time, moaning, weaving a sinuous thread
from childhood to womanhood with her body in his mind,
    telling him her lines about who broke the record,
but only to please—which is why, also aiming to please,
    he gives another little corrective to her now,

        a source of so much new music, the "attack" as right
as a needle in a groove—and they do go around, spinning
        together so nicely, calling it dancing, a sound
activity, like her little games, her white or black lies
        that she's shaved, hairless all over, before he sees
for himself, of course: all cause enough for punishment.

There's the music the spheres make, as there's a music
    her ears make, squeaking beneath his tongue inside
the channels of her head, each orifice ready to accept
    any device. "Is this a form of punishment," he jokes,
"or a discovery of discography? Though it may be hard
    to make out clearly at first, this music is called,

    Duet for Strings and Ropes, played on the lyre
at the base of your torso, the face your hips make,
    sweet sounds leaving your lips as I bend you in half
on my lap, administer the shaft, hands around each calf—
    and your pliant, taut buttocks, your skin echoes back
with a new rhythmic action across your thighs and ass . . ."

After the movement is over, she still rides his penis—
    and all that's essential for his intimate happiness
is that he untie her and let her come to him and sit
    over his face. There he awaits the sweet sounds
of her water: that sluice of thick juice's her song,
    just what he's been waiting to hear all along.

    First, she squats and offers flatness, off-key—
but soon he hears a richer water-music, and lies
    at her feet to drink in the smell and the taste
of her pee like a true connoisseur, swirling it around
    on his tongue as they dance in rhythm to crescendo
together in a new duet of dripping sweat to the end.

The White Room

When the young dancer stood, pale feet exposed
on the high platform at the room's dead center,
"He'd rather stare at my unbound feet forever
than ever hold them in his hands," she thought—
but the old man paid her well to come and pose,
enough for her and her family's whole support.

While those feet flew through fluid arabesques
against sweat-darkened wood, ethereal and fine,
their movements seemed outside of common time:
she held the spinning earth with perfect grace—
until death felt imminent in his caught breaths,
his weak heart halting as she filled that space.

At night he saw her stride the world and crush
his chest beneath the weight of fixed desires:
in his dreams she was a pure, clear atmosphere,
though he gasped for air when translucent skin
on feet and limbs freed from beneath thin plush
descended, as if from a kind of heaven, to him.

For her, it was like a great romance, performed
against bare whitewashed walls, her main design
to marry him, and leave that stark room behind:
so, each new dance became her mute expression,
a plea to be released through him, transformed
beyond the rest of his untouched possessions.

For months then, every other day, she'd come
and play, each time, the shy, naïve coquette
who tried to achieve her exquisite pirouettes
on naked feet at his request—still surprised
to think she held such power over that dumb
and shrunken man with downcast mournful eyes.

One day, she loosened her garments, uncertain,
and watched him watching, under strict control.
Then, he reached for those disembodied clothes
while he saw revealed there, as never before,
tremors of tensions as she held her position—
until she fell, in a deep faint, to the floor.

For a moment it seemed no further breaths came—
but then he drew out a knife, long and thick,
and cut into her flesh, so smooth, so quick,
she didn't wake while her feet were released.
And he didn't wait to watch her blood drain
as he escaped, treasures pressed to his chest.

The girl was found alive within his gardens,
where she had dragged herself to cry for help.
The man was found down a long-abandoned well
at the edge of the estate after three nights,
his bloated white body floating in darkness,
arms reaching up before the searchers' lights:

each hand still held a blackened, rotting foot.
And the girl became quite famous for awhile:
there was much public sympathy for her role,
her need to dance for the sake of her family—
even marriage proposals, though none made good
despite all the reports of her great beauty.

THE EARTHLY PARADISE

"Is it only in the mind of God?"

He used to try to comprehend
the world's geography, to contain
the whole creation—ponds, lakes, streams

growing into rivers' patternings,
flowing to oceans, blue through green—
but now he sees that paradise

rests beyond the edge of that dream,
transcending what can be seen
between thick shades of vegetation

forming constant broken designs,
deltas swelling out into gulfs
of grandeur, circles coming together

to form a charmed circumference—
like the city he was born in,
its defined spaces, margins, clear lines,

which, if held totally in mind,
would be the map of his desire
to inhabit and understand

the anarchic harmony of
its unpremeditated plan
and all his love for this world.

Words Instead Of A Thousand Pictures

A Centaur holds up the newly flayed
skin of a lion while trampling a man
whose whole face is sheared away
from the marble of the Parthenon:

"Even stone rots," stone seems to say,
with all the old meanings that men
still try to retrieve, to preserve
their flesh burned by light into air.

Classical remnants no longer serve
to keep the straitened earth we share,
yet, wrestling on the heads of pins,
trying to save whatever they mean,

we carve our own grave accents on
their uncertainties, like everything
whose broken pieces of marbled skin
define our faces' fates, being human.

TOURISTS UNDER GLASS

They grin at solemn heads with laurel wreaths
calcified to mottled rock, lopsided, bent—
yet want to wrap themselves like thin gold leaf
around each skull left pregnant with intent:

those underwater stares in sepulchres,
with veins of darkness cutting through the bones,
the brains; those perfect teeth in gaping jaws,
adrift in aisles of semi-precious stones.

They see the hand of John the Baptist kept,
a bit of sallow skin and withered flesh,
encased in gold and jewels in Istanbul—

and come to know the ways that skeletons
articulate themselves in tombs, museums
grown up around them, glassed-in, beautiful.

OF THE WORLD

of Cain and Abel, and the grounds
of our inheritance, let pundits beware:
though we still see men stoning each other
    with ever heavier, deadlier rounds,

if God's punishment fits the crime,
in earth's prison, are we all murderers?
How else do Eden's vistas, stretched under
    lush leaves, bloom to tangled vines?

In the cases of those primal apes,
there's something twisted, mysterious
about the ways their lines came down to us
    to walk the earth in the first place.

As we look back at them from afar,
do others' deadly acts explain our lives,
or do we just whittle them down to our size?
    Who'll provide the clarity of stars?

Since holy wars seem as inevitable
as new religious rituals, men's familiar
false handshakes now make all these similar
    endings in blood comprehensible.

OLD COLLABORATORS

Those few who collaborated self-consciously
with killers through one-way mirrors darkly

have learned the equivalencies of either/or
propositions: how they resemble forevermore

the characters they assumed, as secretaries,
book-keepers, coolly anonymous apothecaries,

changing the names until no useful memories
might emerge, no messages for their enemies—

until the time when they let those lives go,
their funeral corteges grey as trodden snow.

AT "THE WHITE TOWER," THESSALONIKI

Is there any spot left of uncontested soil,
where no one's spilled another man's blood?
Though it may seem superstitious to shrink
from this specific place of former torture,

we can still lend ourselves to some stance
of resistance by insisting now on defining
our private worlds as opposed to the world,
this earth as an historical killing ground,

thus judiciously introducing new languages
where previous ones are permitted to lapse,
like the fading harbor lights trailing off
in a cool bay at certain angles to the sun

coming to rest in a still-bloodied stretch
that marks the simple pathway to this door.

VISITING KASSANDRA

Sick and tired of feeling sick and tired, victims
of the daily grinds no visions warmed, but warned,
they read, knowing reigns may soon be ended, born:
"This world needs to be seen with oracles' wisdom."

If they entered that future, beyond all the smoke
and mirrors, would it be the old lives they saved,
or would pallid caverns once thought a god's cave
proclaim innocence over before some fatal strokes?

Getting there was enough for a couple who'd drive
to the Kassandra peninsula just to see that shore:
coming close, never even getting out of their car,
it was sufficient to know they never could arrive.

The sun was shining then through the big blue bay
windows, out over the bay, cutting into half-haze.

WEST HIGHLAND LINE

They rode up one Sunday and saw God
in water, rock, sky: broken off clods
rode rough waves in the lochs; twisted roots,
the remains of ancient pine forests,
lay exposed, agonized skeletons

among pale stones washed down from mountains
now barren of all but matted shrouds
of wild grass blowing beneath low clouds—
moors broken only by loam-clogged streams
cutting through bogs filled with broken forms.

Are peninsular peoples insular?
Out from their Crucifixions stared
louts and churls, grinning or grimacing
at Christ's Passion portrayed in paintings
brute Nature will someday roll back over:

glaciers under constant grinding pressure
restoring the works of men to the earth;
thick mists filled with the perfume of death;
cliffs breaking off into roiling bays—
bones raised in the bleached bloom of those days.

LITTLE STAR OF BETHLEHEM

Suppose there's a greater river
of galaxies hurtling through
the emptiness of Space, drawn
by undiscovered forces towards
this corner of the universe,
and all we need are eyes enough
to see, or instruments to know
the gravity in everything.

We have ears that cannot hear;
we have mouths, but we can't tell
tales tall enough to sound alarms
to villagers who still believe
in Santa Claus, abandoned towns—
needing a hand to write dreams down,
snoring in beds while waiting for
true belief's corroborations.

Suppose that proofs like cosmic rays
surround us all, yet we can't find
the senses to make sense of them:
what clues they leave may only be
sleights of sleigh-rides, fantasies,
a slight suggestion treading roofs
with a fat sack and reindeer hoofs,
imaginary, becoming "real."

Then, open-eyed, we'll wake to see
new havoc wreaked about the house,
torn packaging, gift paper wrap,
ribbons strewn along the floors
where children cry among the mass
of sleepy relatives who wait
like everyone else for a day
unlike any other, so they say.

Suppose there are pathways laid
throughout the dark, while, overhead,
chimneys of lit houses hold
good children's wishes for new toys,
wanting saving from that great void
projected to the ends of days,
and somehow we'll be saved. Why not?
Such wonders have happened before.

THE ANIMA

Now that he's lived in one place so long,
stepping over successive underlings,
he becomes nostalgic at the smell
of wet air at the changes of seasons,
sometimes even feels an adamant
anima start to stir and come out:
"It may be a puzzle to you," she says,

"but the damned don't change: they just hang around,
slinking inside, never facing their fears
of being constantly rebuked." Accused,
he averts his eyes from the problem
of disbelief in himself, his simple
daily resistance to the evidence
of what he's inexorably become:

"You've less than half a lifetime to forgive
the demands of the monstrous diamonds
others mine from your desires. Hard, white,
blazing out to the air, one brilliant stone
left inside your chest may save you now.
It continues to glow, casts a bountiful
shadow: why don't you come in under it?"

As if in agreement, he starts pointing
around his room like an auctioneer
of his paltry effects, a broken man
bidding off the collections of his life
for some small return, wanting the heavy
loads of remembrance taken off his hands,
sad items strangers might buy up or trash.

A muse might intervene when angels won't:
he wishes her tongue, touching his, won't parch
even as she places her finger to his lips,
calmly calling forth new hungry waves.

A SOUL

In mirrors, we see how people invent
their gods because they desire to be
those gods themselves. To see every
sparrow fall. To have that infinite

imagination in which even the random
movements of leaves or birds, moment
by moment, as they fill new branches
and empty branches, might come clear.

That wisdom. As if we could ever be
definitively there, flying, climbing
within conceiving winds to the fruit
of the tree, maintaining its mystery:

a little patch of ground and gravity
all the small universe we might need
to plot the grounds of our occasions,
to see, within the shelter of an eye,

a soul.

In Autumn

He returns to another world
with its heaving gutturals,
the Russian language inside
his head, whenever he reads
or stares at a blank square
of sky out of train windows
as he did autumn afternoons
when he was young, the blue
houses flowing by like wood
boxes on the waves of grain
in flood before they froze,
those ancient golden shapes
informing aging dreams upon
the Trans-Siberian Express.

Today, wherever he may wake
along a small town sidewalk
or lie in bed with the ache
of blue days floating past,
he squints deep into a cold
sun drowning the old houses
sunk in tundra at the edges
of empty steppes stretching
into a shimmering afternoon
like mirages from the train
buried up to its windows in
snow and steam, bobbing
like breaths on the horizon
of the otherwise clear sky.

SILENCE

For a moment there is silence,
disconnected from your tongue
still talking, as if the color
orange were abstracted from
its source—the fruit before us
lying emptied on the table—
and there were only a rind
of sound, nothing in its place.

Then voice returns to your lips,
which keep moving over the taste
of *orange*, the word on the air
as intense as that bright color
forming in mist before your face—
and all sounds seem orange now
as they leave your open mouth,
becoming a cloud of silence.

THE POEM

They'd never heard of such whiteness
as that sweet blank piece of paper
he called "The Compassionate Buddha."

He lived by himself in that poem,
which called them—and like that page, in time,
they've come to rest beneath its sheer net.

FIGURES IN THE CARPETS

[Sarouk]

We buy what we cannot control, the rugs,
    rhythm-makers, containing refrains of
the oldest story: a man takes a journey.
    I have no stories inside me, he says,
so travels on, to rest beneath a carpet
    of blue constellations, star patterns
at the edges of disordered border walls.
    At the center, a meditative medallion
makes a moving immortal-flowered ground:
    to live there is to give oneself over
to greenness, redness, occasional blues,
    holding those spirits of woolen dyes
rising from the knots within to breathe
    against the woven, multi-colored air.

[Bidjar]

Now there is a coat of many colors hung
    around the wanderer's shoulders where
he climbs out from that pit, down which
    he flung himself, or was thrown into.
Reaching to soothe his wounds, he finds
    the dusts of centuries residing there
beneath his feet, the hopeful travelers
    passing, wearing thin, fighting about
how best to articulate the names of gods
    for whom they yearn—accursed by wars'
helmet curves, shields, chained stitches
    of unmediated reds and yellowed husks
of blood—broken lines marking a garden
    in whose precincts his journey began.

[Kazak]

Three sunbursts spin, enigmatic energies
    through golden cloudbanks, surrounding
latchhooks; three eagles, darting within
    these shifting images: they return him
to streets of lit porches in summer dark,
    a boy stuttering over random syllables,
a blindfolded man pleading for his life—
    whose fate is in the hands of some men
whose fate is in the hands of other men,
    whose fate... until the whole pattern
emerges, and the language becomes clear.
    On the floor lies his mother, moaning,
until he comes out, guilty, before her—
    amid the mud of his own frozen blood.

[Shirvan]

To live inside such squares as the weaver
    of this green, becoming golden, labor;
to pull back old skins and try to emerge,
    victorious, from that old prison after
so many years, is to find a path back to
    harmonious designs, surely centered on
the search—yet still speaking of a life
    with knotted figures seen as suffering
variations on themes that can be inferred
    from small vibrations of weft and warp,
the "snakes" within the threads worn down
    to the shapes of ribbons, even rhythms
writhing in a loom of days: those humming
    ancient instruments whose music seems

[Shiraz]

raw as colors governed by the earth, pink
    as brick, or deserts scraped from rock,
rough clay slowly grinding, then drifting
    down the slopes of the central plateaus
to fresh respites from thinner regions of
    desiccation fixed at the fringes below.
These lands lie under the ache of desire,
    which calls feet out to play upon sand,
to fill each new hollow, and dance about,
    tongues turning on the knots of umber,
ochre, woven into those undulating waves
    others might summon in flowery manners
to escape from bitter orange, still held
    by recalcitrant fingers, to the purple

[Kerman]

empowering all those who try to hold on—
    as all things will hold to themselves
an idea of themselves—to an aspiration
    towards good fortune, unwavering even
unto death. Yet here are dusky passages,
    canopies of clearness, an everlasting
understanding of the earth as cancerous
    points of coloration, acid starbursts,
or dangerous blots—all blurring the way
    to move past sight: perspectives lost,
and found again, symmetrical, surrounded
    by the mementos one saves from travel,
old friends, like hues that may betoken,
    in hopefulness, some changes of heart.

[Senneh]

This creates a powerful language about
   how to levitate a plane—for even as
the occasional murmurs of new machines
   are heard in the land, as old cyclic
gardens arrange themselves in the whorls
   and tendrils throughout tilled fields,
snakes hold up this world in variations
   of light blue skies above temptation.
Even when an illiterate weaver mistakes
   an old date for the design, then dyes
and binds strange numbers into a ground,
   the change of the serif, for instance,
in a calligraphy of days marks the date
   of a cartouche as mysterious, unknown.

[Kashan]

Yet the signals from the borders suggest
   a different tale: lozenges are bottles
strewn along mauve and terra cotta roads,
   shaped like a woman found lying along
the side of those same roads—the figure
   of flesh, going nowhere but endlessly
back on itself—as a web of years frames
   a dying kind of certitude, innocence.
The birds in these cages signify singing,
   as the tapestries of perfected threads
suggest reticence, chosen intermediaries
   to the indeterminacy of all creation:
and we can buy it yet, articulate or not,
   with each new freeing of our hearts.

CARNEGIE MELLON POETRY SERIES

1975
The Living and the Dead, Ann Hayes
In the Face of Descent, T. Alan Broughton

1976
The Week the Dirigible Came, Jay Meek
Full of Lust and Good Usage, Stephen Dunn

1977
How I Escaped from the Labyrinth and Other Poems, Philip Dacey
The Lady from the Dark Green Hills, Jim Hall
For Luck: Poems 1962-1977, H.L. Van Brunt
By the Wreckmaster's Cottage, Paula Rankin

1978
New & Selected Poems, James Bertolino
The Sun Fetcher, Michael Dennis Browne
A Circus of Needs, Stephen Dunn
The Crowd Inside, Elizabeth Libbey

1979
Paying Back the Sea, Philip Dow
Swimmer in the Rain, Robert Wallace
Far from Home, T. Alan Broughton
The Room Where Summer Ends, Peter Cooley
No Ordinary World, Mekeel McBride

1980
And the Man Who Was Traveling Never Got Home, H.L. Van Brunt
Drawing on the Walls, Jay Meek
The Yellow House on the Corner, Rita Dove
The 8-Step Grapevine, Dara Wier
The Mating Reflex, Jim Hall

1981
A Little Faith, John Skoyles
Augers, Paula Rankin
Walking Home from the Icehouse, Vern Rutsala
Work and Love, Stephen Dunn

The Rote Walker, Mark Jarman
Morocco Journal, Richard Harteis
Songs of a Returning Soul, Elizabeth Libbey

1982
The Granary, Kim R. Stafford
Calling the Dead, C.G. Hanzlicek
Dreams Before Sleep, T. Alan Broughton
Sorting It Out, Anne S. Perlman
Love Is Not a Consolation; It Is a Light, Primus St. John

1983
The Going Under of the Evening Land, Mekeel McBride
Museum, Rita Dove
Air and Salt, Eve Shelnutt
Nightseasons, Peter Cooley

1984
Falling from Stardom, Jonathan Holden
Miracle Mile, Ed Ochester
Girlfriends and Wives, Robert Wallace
Earthly Purposes, Jay Meek
Not Dancing, Stephen Dunn
The Man in the Middle, Gregory Djanikian
A Heart Out of This World, David James
All You Have in Common, Dara Wier

1985
Smoke from the Fires, Michael Dennis Browne
Full of Lust and Good Usage, Stephen Dunn (2nd edition)
Far and Away, Mark Jarman
Anniversary of the Air, Michael Waters
To the House Ghost, Paula Rankin
Midwinter Transport, Anne Bromley

1986
Seals in the Inner Harbor, Brendan Galvin
Thomas and Beulah, Rita Dove
Further Adventures With You, C.D. Wright
Fifteen to Infinity, Ruth Fainlight
False Statements, Jim Hall
When There Are No Secrets, C.G. Hanzlicek

1987

Some Gangster Pain, Gillian Conoley
Other Children, Lawrence Raab
Internal Geography, Richard Harteis
The Van Gogh Notebook, Peter Cooley
A Circus of Needs, Stephen Dunn (2nd edition)
Ruined Cities, Vern Rutsala
Places and Stories, Kim R. Stafford

1988

Preparing to Be Happy, T. Alan Broughton
Red Letter Days, Mekeel McBride
The Abandoned Country, Thomas Rabbitt
The Book of Knowledge, Dara Wier
Changing the Name to Ochester, Ed Ochester
Weaving the Sheets, Judith Root

1989

Recital in a Private Home, Eve Shelnutt
A Walled Garden, Michael Cuddihy
The Age of Krypton, Carol J. Pierman
Land That Wasn't Ours, David Keller
Stations, Jay Meek
The Common Summer: New and Selected Poems, Robert Wallace
The Burden Lifters, Michael Waters
Falling Deeply into America, Gregory Djanikian
Entry in an Unknown Hand, Franz Wright

1990

Why the River Disappears, Marcia Southwick
Staying Up For Love, Leslie Adrienne Miller
Dreamer, Primus St. John

1991

Permanent Change, John Skoyles
Clackamas, Gary Gildner
Tall Stranger, Gillian Conoley
The Gathering of My Name, Cornelius Eady
A Dog in the Lifeboat, Joyce Peseroff
Raised Underground, Renate Wood
Divorce: A Romance, Paula Rankin

1992
Modern Ocean, James Harms
The Astonished Hours, Peter Cooley
You Won't Remember This, Michael Dennis Browne
Twenty Colors, Elizabeth Kirschner
First A Long Hesitation, Eve Shelnutt
Bountiful, Michael Waters
Blue for the Plough, Dara Wier
All That Heat in a Cold Sky, Elizabeth Libbey

1993
Trumpeter, Jeannine Savard
Cuba, Ricardo Pau-Llosa
The Night World and the Word Night, Franz Wright
The Book of Complaints, Richard Katrovas

1994
If Winter Come: Collected Poems, 1967–1992, Alvin Aubert
Of Desire and Disorder, Wayne Dodd
Ungodliness, Leslie Adrienne Miller
Rain, Henry Carlile
Windows, Jay Meek
A Handful of Bees, Dzvinia Orlowsky

1995
Germany, Caroline Finkelstein
Housekeeping in a Dream, Laura Kasischke
About Distance, Gregory Djanikian
Wind of the White Dresses, Mekeel McBride
Above the Tree Line, Kathy Mangan
In the Country of Elegies, T. Alan Broughton
Scenes from the Light Years, Anne C. Bromley
Quartet, Angela Ball
Rorschach Test, Franz Wright

1996
Back Roads, Patricia Henley
Dyer's Thistle, Peter Balakian
Beckon, Gillian Conoley
The Parable of Fire, James Reiss
Cold Pluto, Mary Ruefle
Orders of Affection, Arthur Smith

Colander, Michael McFee

1997
Growing Darkness, Growing Light, Jean Valentine
Selected Poems, 1965-1995, Michael Dennis Browne
Your Rightful Childhood: New and Selected Poems, Paula Rankin
Headlands: New and Selected Poems, Jay Meek
Soul Train, Allison Joseph
The Autobiography of a Jukebox, Cornelius Eady
The Patience of the Cloud Photographer, Elizabeth Holmes
Madly in Love, Aliki Barnstone
An Octave Above Thunder: New and Selected Poems, Carol Muske

1998
Yesterday Had a Man In It, Leslie Adrienne Miller
Definition of the Soul, John Skoyles
Dithyrambs, Richard Katrovas
Postal Routes, Elizabeth Kirschner
The Blue Salvages, Wayne Dodd
The Joy Addict, James Harms
Clemency and Other Poems, Colette Inez
Scattering the Ashes, Jeff Friedman
Sacred Conversations, Peter Cooley
Life Among the Trolls, Maura Stanton

1999
Justice, Caroline Finkelstein
Edge of House, Dzvinia Orlowsky
A Thousand Friends of Rain:
    New and Selected Poems, 1976-1998, Kim Stafford
The Devil's Child, Fleda Brown Jackson
World as Dictionary, Jesse Lee Kercheval
Vereda Tropical, Ricardo Pau-Llosa
The Museum of the Revolution, Angela Ball
Our Master Plan, Dara Wier

2000
Small Boat with Oars of Different Size, Thom Ward
Post Meridian, Mary Ruefle
Hierarchies of Rue, Roger Sauls
Constant Longing, Dennis Sampson
Mortal Education, Joyce Peseroff